Bodies of Water

Rivers and Streams

Cassie Mayer

www.heinemann.co.uk/library
Visit our website to find out more information about Heinemann Library books.

To order:
 Phone 44 (0) 1865 888066
Send a fax to 44 (0) 1865 314091
Visit the Heinemann Bookshop at www.heinemann.co.uk/library to browse our
 catalogue and order online.

First published in Great Britain by Heinemann Library,
Halley Court, Jordan Hill, Oxford OX2 8EJ, part of Harcourt
Education. Heinemann is a registered trademark of Harcourt
Education Ltd.

Editorial: Diyan Leake and Cassie Mayer
Design: Joanna Hinton-Malivoire
Picture research: Erica Martin
Production: Duncan Gilbert

Originated by Chroma Graphics (Overseas) Pte Ltd
Printed and bound in China by South China Printing Co. Ltd

ISBN 978 0 4311 8471 5

11 10 09 08 07
10 9 8 7 6 5 4 3 2 1

British Library Cataloguing in Publication Data
Mayer, Cassie
Bodies of Water: Rivers and Streams

A full catalogue record for this book is available from the
British Library

Acknowledgements
The publishers would like to thank the following for permission
to reproduce photographs: Brand X Images pp. **8, 12,
back cover**; Corbis pp. **4** (NASA), **17** (David Muench),
18 (B.S.P.I.), **19** (photocuisine/Gauter), **20** (Buddy Mays),
21 (Free Agents Limited), **23** (rice field: B.S.P.I.; cargo
ship: Buddy Mays); Getty Images pp. **5** (Photonica/Bridget
Webber), **6** (Iconica/David Zimmerman), **7** (LOOK/Florian
Werner), **9** (The Image Bank/Preston Schlebusch), **11**
(Purestock), **13** (George Kavanagh), **14** (Photodisc);
Nature Picture Library p. **16** (Kim Taylor); Punchstock p. **10**
(UpperCut Images); Robert Harding p. **15** (Travel Library).

Cover photograph reproduced with permission of Jupiter
Images/Workbook Stock (David Collier).

Every effort has been made to contact copyright holders
of any material reproduced in this book. Any omissions will
be rectified in subsequent printings if notice is given to the
publishers.

Contents

Rivers

water

Most of the Earth is covered by water.

river

Some of this water is in rivers.

A river is water that flows across land.
Rivers flow to the sea.

River water is not salty.

It is called fresh water.

Streams

A stream is a very small river.

Most streams start up in the hills.

Streams may run into rivers.

How rivers form

Rainwater runs down a mountain.
Rainwater forms streams.

When streams join together, they make a river.

Rivers wash away soil.

Rivers can even wash away rocks.

Rivers can form valleys.

Where rivers end

Some rivers flow into the ocean.

Some rivers flow into lakes.

River life

There are many animals in rivers.

There are many plants in rivers.

How we use rivers

Farmers use rivers to water crops.

River water is cleaned.

Then it goes through pipes to our taps.

Some rivers are very deep.

Big boats can carry goods on rivers.

People can go on river journeys to
see different places.

River facts

The Nile is the longest river in the world. It is in Africa.

The Mississippi River is the largest river in North America.

Picture glossary

crop a plant that is grown for something, such as food

goods things that people buy and sell

Index

Notes for parents and teachers

Before reading

Ask the children if they have seen a river. What did it look like? Was the water deep or shallow? Look at pictures of rivers and streams. Can they tell you the difference between a river and a stream?

After reading

Can water flow uphill? Put some water in a washing-up bowl. Place or ramp in the bowl. Ask the children to pour the water from the top of the ramp. What happens? If they pour water at the bottom of the ramp, does the water go up?

Stream song. Sing the song "Row, row, row your boat / Gently down the stream / Merrily, merrily, merrily, merrily / Life is but a dream." Some children could pretend to row their boats. Other children could pretend they were swimming in a river.

River poster. Encourage the class to draw a river starting as streams in the mountains and then becoming a river going to the sea. Draw and cut out the plants and animals they might see along a river bank or in the river. Label and display the poster.